Science Experiments

WEATHER

by
John Farndon

BENCHMARK BOOKS

MARSHALL CAVENDISH
NEW YORK

Marshall Cavendish Corporation

99 White Plains Road

Tarrytown, New York 10591

© Marshall Cavendish Corporation, 2001

Created by Brown Partworks Ltd

Library of Congress Cataloging-in-Publication Data

Farndon, John

    Weather / by John Farndon
      p. cm. — (Science experiments)
      Includes index.
      Summary: A collection of experiments that explore the nature of
weather and how it is measured and examined.
      ISBN 0-7614-1089-9 (lib. bdg.)
      1. Weather—Experiments—Juvenile literature. [1. Weather—
Experiments. 2. Meteorology—Experiments. 3. Experiments.]
I. Title.
QC981.3 F37 2001   99-089261
551.6'078—dc21

Printed in Hong Kong

PHOTOGRAPHIC CREDITS

t – top; b – bottom; c – center; l – left; r – right

Corbis: title page, Robert Landau (c); p4, Darrell Gulin (b); p10, Robert
Landau (br); p12, Ann Purcell (bl)
David Noble: p9, (tl)
Ecoscene: p20, 21 Wayne Lawler (b); p21, Glover (bc)
The Image Bank: p16, 17 Eric Meola (b); p24, A.T.Willett (br)
Papilio: p21, (cr); p21, (c)
SPL: p7, Jerry Mason (tr)
Travel Ink: p21, Ken Gibson (br)

Step-by-step photography throughout: Martin Norris

Front cover: Martin Norris

Contents

THE ROLE OF THE SUN

The Sun gives off energy that helps things grow. If the Sun is high in the sky it is generally warmer than when the Sun is low, near the horizon.

Every minute, enough sunshine hits each single square yard (square meter) of Earth's surface to boil a big pan of water. The coldest temperature recorded on Earth is –126°F (–88°C) in Antarctica, but without sunshine, the whole Earth would be much, much colder all the time.

The amount of heat coming from the Sun never varies and is called the "solar constant." But not all the world is warmed equally. The equator and the tropics (on either side of the equator) face the Sun more or less directly all the time, which is why the Sun climbs high in the sky at midday if you are near the equator. This keeps the tropics very warm all year round. But places toward the poles only face the Sun at an angle, and so the Sun is never very high in the sky. This is why the polar regions are always cold and covered in ice.

In focus

MOVING EARTH

Although the Sun appears to move through the sky, it is really Earth (and therefore you) that moves. The Sun seems to rise and fall day by day as Earth turns you around to face it more or less directly. Shadows are shortest at midday, when Earth turns you to face the Sun most directly. They are longest at sunrise and sunset and in winter, when, if you are in northern parts of the northern hemisphere, you are at such an angle to the Sun that it is almost hidden behind the horizon.

The height of the Sun in the sky varies with the seasons because as Earth orbits (circles) around the Sun, it is always tilted in the same direction. When Earth is on one side of the Sun, the northern hemisphere (the half of the world north of the equator) is tilted toward the Sun, bringing summer. At the same time, the southern hemisphere is tilted away and so it is winter. Six months later, Earth has circled to the other side of the Sun, and the seasons are reversed.

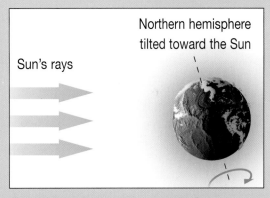

Summer in the northern hemisphere.

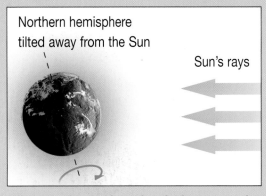

Winter in the northern hemisphere.

HOW TO MAKE A SUNDIAL

Before you begin

Get an adult to drill a hole to fit the pencil toward one corner of a square of wood.

You will need

✔ A square piece of plywood with a hole in one corner

✔ A marker or pen

✔ A protractor

✔ A pencil

✔ A ruler

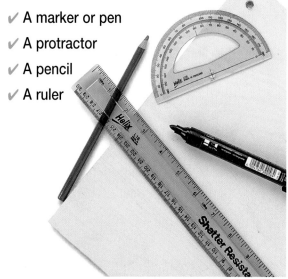

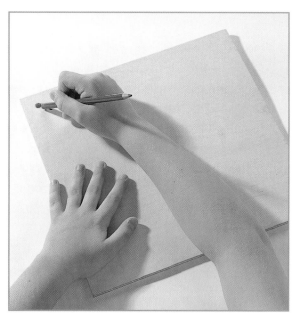

1 Fit the pencil in the hole. Place the board on the ground outdoors with the pencil toward the midday Sun.

What is happening?

The power of the Sun to warm depends on how directly it shines down on the ground. The higher it is, on the whole, the hotter it gets.

The sundial lets you measure how long the shadow is through the day as the Sun rises at dawn, climbs to midday, and then sinks again at sunset.

You can see the variation from season to season, with the Sun highest (shadows shortest) in summer. You can also use the sundial to tell the time on a sunny day.

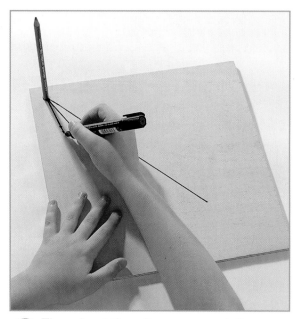

3 Thoughout the afternoon, mark the shadow at hourly intervals. The lines will fan out from the pencil.

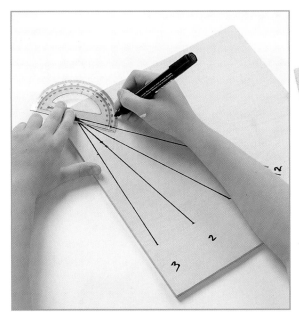

In the real world

You can feel the difference between a cool day and a hot day, but for exact measurement you need a thermometer. Meteorologists (who study weather) use special maximum and minimum thermometers. One side shows the maximum temperature reached since the last reading; the other shows the minimum. An ordinary household thermometer will do for simple daily readings. Measure the temperature, in the shade, at the same time every day.

2 At exactly midday on a sunny day (when shadows are shortest), mark a line along the shadow of the pencil.

Now you can tell the time from the direction of the pencil's shadow when the weather is sunny.

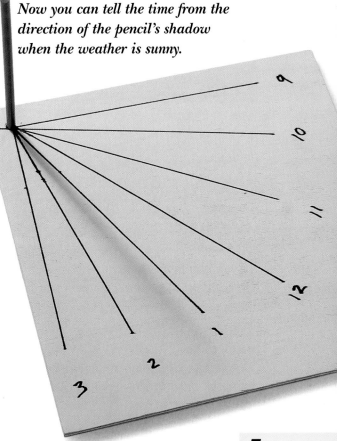

4 Use the protractor to measure the angles. Mark and draw lines for the time in the morning at the same angles.

HOW LIGHT CHANGES

You will need

- ✔ A drinking glass
- ✔ A teaspoon
- ✔ A flashlight
- ✔ Water
- ✔ Milk

1 Fill the glass with water. Then add about a teaspoonful of milk—just enough to make the water slightly cloudy.

What is happening?

When you shine the flashlight through the milky liquid, some of the color in the light is absorbed. A similar thing happens to sunlight. At sunset, for example, the sunlight has to travel farther to reach us. Most of the blue light is scattered by particles in the atmosphere. The red passes through, so the sky looks red. A polluted atmosphere (with a lot of particles) scatters all but the red sunlight.

2 Shine the flashlight on the glass. You will see that the light reflected from the milk particles has a blue tinge.

In the real world

Skies are blue because the gas molecules in the air reflect the Sun. But dust, water, and other particles dilute the blue by reflecting other colors. So skies are bluest when the air is purest. In the northern hemisphere, skies are typically bluest when bright sunshine on a clear day in mid-morning combines with a strong northerly wind, which sweeps the atmosphere clean and dries the air out as it moves to the warmer south.

Rainbows appear when sunlight hits a shower of rain: each drop splits the sunlight into the seven colors that make up white light, and the drops reflect the light back to your eye.

3 If you now shine the flashlight through the glass from behind, it will look yellow, like the Sun during the day.

4 If you add more milk, the light becomes pinker, as bluer colors are absorbed. Try using different liquids in the glass.

WINDS AND HOW THEY BLOW

On a windy day you can see how the air moves by flying a kite. The kite catches the wind and ducks and dives in the eddies.

Did you know?

In 1805, a British sea captain called Francis Beaufort began to measure winds by counting how many sails ships could safely use. He divided winds into 13 "forces" from calm to hurricane. Even though meteorologists (weather scientists) now measure winds with accurate meters, Beaufort's scale is still used to classify winds.

Gentle or fierce, all winds start the same way. Air moves because the Sun warms some places more than others, creating differences in air pressure, which push the air about. As the Sun moves through the sky, it heats some parts of the sea and land more than others. The warmth heats the air above, making it expand and become lighter, so it begins to rise. Elsewhere, the air is cool and dense, so it sinks. Winds blow because air is squeezed out from beneath the cool, sinking air and drawn in under the rising warm air.

Some winds blow in one place, and have a local name, such as the Chinook in North America and the Mistral in southern France.

Others are part of a huge circulation pattern that sends winds over the entire globe and creates persistent winds called prevailing winds.

In focus

WINDS AROUND EARTH

Winds may seem chaotic, but there is a pattern to the main winds, which is set by Earth's rotation and the heat of the Sun. Winds do not blow in a straight line between the poles and the equator but are pushed at an angle by the spinning of Earth. This is called the Coriolis effect. The pole-to-equator flow is split into three zones: the polar regions, mid-latitudes, and tropics.

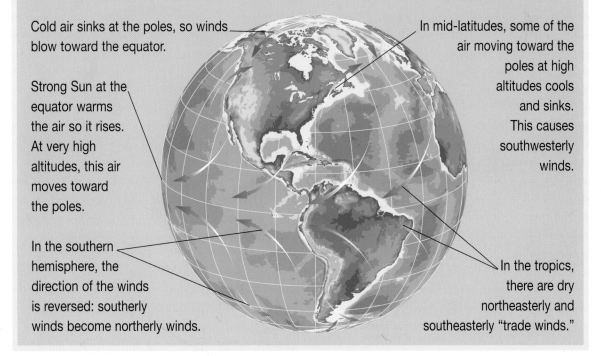

Cold air sinks at the poles, so winds blow toward the equator.

Strong Sun at the equator warms the air so it rises. At very high altitudes, this air moves toward the poles.

In the southern hemisphere, the direction of the winds is reversed: southerly winds become northerly winds.

In mid-latitudes, some of the air moving toward the poles at high altitudes cools and sinks. This causes southwesterly winds.

In the tropics, there are dry northeasterly and southeasterly "trade winds."

MAKING A MOBILE

You will need

- ✔ A square sheet of thin plastic
- ✔ A lid or plate to draw around
- ✔ A needle and cotton thread
- ✔ Re-usable poster putty
- ✔ A marker pen
- ✔ Scissors
- ✔ An awl

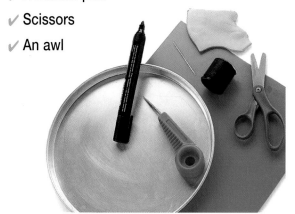

1 Place the lid in the center of the plastic sheet, face downward. Use the marker to trace a circle around it.

In the real world

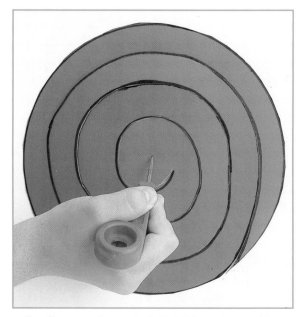

Thermals provide the lift needed by glider pilots and birds for flying. Glider pilots look for cumulus clouds because they indicate the presence of updrafts, which often form over plowed fields, bare soil, and large concrete areas such as airports—though they are also found over cold water such as lakes. Some birds can detect the presence of electrical changes produced by thermals.

3 Cut out the spiral, finishing about ½ in (1 cm) from the center. Make a hole through the center with the awl.

2 Mark the center of the circle and, starting from the outer edge, draw a smooth spiral about ½ in (1 cm) wide.

4 Thread a length of cotton through the hole and knot it firmly. Use the poster putty to hang the spiral over a radiator.

What is happening?

Outside, the Sun warms surfaces, and the surfaces warm the air, which rises. The rising currents of warm air are called thermals. In this experiment, the heat to create the thermal comes from the radiator, rather than from the Sun.

Watch the spiral begin to turn in the rising warm air current. The rising air pushes the snake around.

MAKING A WEATHER VANE

You will need

✔ Two strong plastic drinking straws

✔ A small flower pot

✔ Re-usable poster putty

✔ A magnetic compass

✔ A sheet of thin card

✔ A wooden skewer

✔ A marker pen

✔ A compass

✔ Scissors

✔ A pencil

✔ A ruler

1 Cut out a triangle of card about 2 in (5 cm) deep and 3 in (7.5 cm) across the base. Cut it in two across the middle.

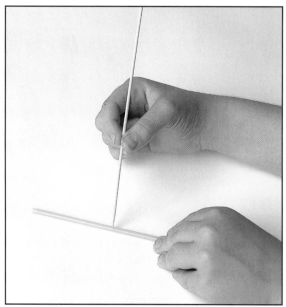

3 Push the wooden skewer through the middle of the straw, very slightly nearer the end with the base of the triangle.

4 Mark the base of the pot N (for north), E, S, and W. Place a straw in the hole, holding it in place with poster putty.

2 Cut slots in each end of a straw. Push the top of the triangle into one slot and the base into the slot at the other end.

In the real world

Winds are identified by the direction they blow from. A wind blowing from southwest to northeast is called a southwesterly wind. So a weather vane points not in the direction the wind is blowing but in the direction it is blowing from. The direction a wind is blowing from indicates the kind of weather it might bring. In the United States, for instance, winds from the north bring cold weather, while in Europe, westerly winds bring warm, wet weather.

5 Slot the skewer into the straw. Take the flower pot outdoors and use the compass to align the marks.

Let the arrow swing in the wind until it stays pointing in one direction. The letters show which way the wind is blowing.

TORNADOES AND HURRICANES

Tornadoes and hurricanes are swirling winds with enormous power. Hurricanes form over tropical oceans. They have strong, rotating winds that whirl across the sea. As a hurricane approaches the shore, its fierce winds drive high waves onto the land.

Tornadoes are even more destructive. They form when masses of cold air and warm air try to change places. This produces a twisting motion

Did you know?
One of the strongest recorded hurricanes happened in October, 1893. This giant hurricane hit the Gulf Coast, killing nearly 2,000 people.

A tornado sweeps across farmland, destroying summer crops.

called a vortex. A tornado seems to hang from a thundercloud rather like a massive elephant's trunk. In fact, the air is sweeping upward.

Tornadoes are also called twisters and dust devils. They are the fastest winds on Earth. They sweep across the ground at up to 300 mph (480 km/h), destroying everything in their path. People, animals, trains, automobiles, trailers, and buildings have been caught up by these mighty winds.

In focus

HOW A HURRICANE FORMS

Hurricanes are violent tropical storms. If they form in the western Pacific Ocean, they are called typhoons. Hurricanes that start in the Indian Ocean are called tropical cyclones. The storms form in the same way.

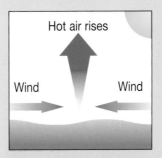

Hurricanes form when areas of low pressure develop over warm seas in the tropics. Air above the sea heats up and rises. Winds rush into the low pressure zone.

As the rising air and winds meet, they circle around. Hurricanes circle counterclockwise in the northern hemisphere and clockwise in the southern hemisphere.

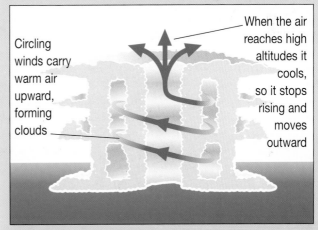

Circling winds carry warm air upward, forming clouds

When the air reaches high altitudes it cools, so it stops rising and moves outward

The hurricane moves over the ocean and continues to suck up warm, moist air. It loses its power if it passes over cool water or land. Hurricanes can measure up to 300 miles (480 km) across, with winds of 75 mph (120 km/h). But the center of the hurricane is calm.

HOW TO MAKE A VORTEX

You will need

- ✔ Two identical large soft drink bottles
- ✔ Food coloring
- ✔ Strong tape
- ✔ Strong foil
- ✔ Scissors
- ✔ An awl

1 Cut a piece of foil large enough to cover the necks of the bottles. Make a hole in the foil with an awl.

3 Fill half the bottle with water. Add some food coloring. This will make it easier to see the vortex.

4 Tape the foil into place over the neck of the bottle. Make sure the hole in the foil is near the center of the neck.

What is happening?

The water forms a vortex, moving in a circular motion like the air currents. At the center there is no water, so it is still, like the calm at the center of a tornado.

2 Hold the foil over the neck of one bottle so that the hole is in the middle. Trim away any extra foil.

Turn the whole thing upside down. As the water flows through the hole it will form a vortex.

To get the vortex started, you may have to swirl the bottles slightly.

5 Hold the two bottles, one on top of the other. Tape the two bottles together, neck to neck, making a watertight seal.

CLOUDS AND HUMIDITY

You might not know it, but you are walking around in a sea of water. Like a sponge, air soaks up invisible water vapor. All air near the ground contains some water vapor, but just how much it holds—the air's humidity—depends on how hot and dry the weather is. Water gets into the air because the

Different shapes of cloud can tell us about the type of weather to expect. Puffy cumulus clouds (like those seen here) generally indicate fair weather. However, the dark layers of altostratus that are forming tell us a depression is approaching.

Did you know?

As the air cools down, it holds less water. After a cool night, leaves and grass are often covered in drops of water that the air could not hold. This is called dew.

Sun heats up oceans and lakes. Millions of gallons of water then rise into the air as water vapor. This process is called evaporation. As the moist air full of water vapor rises, it cools.

Eventually, when the vapor is high in the air, it gets so cool that the moisture turns into a mist of water droplets, or ice crystals if it is very cold. We see these collections of droplets and ice crystals as clouds.

CLOUDS

Clouds come in all shapes and sizes, but all are made of billions of tiny water drops or ice crystals. There are three basic types—fluffy white heaped "cumulus" clouds, huge blanket layers of "stratus" clouds, and wispy "cirrus" clouds.

Weather experts also identify the different clouds according to how high they are in the sky ("cirro-", "alto-", or "nimbo-" for high, medium, or low). So altocumulus clouds, for instance, are fluffy cumulus clouds at medium-high altitude while cirrostratus are high, flat clouds. Some clouds, such as stratocumulus and cirrocumulus ("mackerel" skies) are mixtures of two of the three basic types.

Dark gray rain clouds are given the name nimbus. So nimbostratus are layered rainclouds, while cumulonimbus are huge, piled-up thunderclouds.

Cirrus (high, wispy clouds formed from ice) often warn of storms ahead.

Stratocumulus are layers of cumulus, forming in unsettled weather.

Cumulus may grow into towering clouds if there are rising air currents.

Thundery cumulonimbus, the tallest clouds, often stretch into anvil shapes.

A WET AND DRY HYGROMETER

You will need

✔ Two identical thermometers
✔ Marker pens and ruler
✔ A square of plywood
✔ A spray can lid
✔ Cotton cloth
✔ Balsa wood
✔ A notebook
✔ Glue

1 Position the thermometers on the board, with bulbs level, and use a pen to mark the temperature scale onto the board down one side of each of the thermometers.

Take it further

HUMIDITY READINGS

Scientists have worked out the maximum humidity of the air (the total amount of water vapor it can hold) at different temperatures. They have drawn up charts that show how humid the air is for the different temperature readings on a wet and dry hygrometer. If you have one of these charts (called humidity tables) at school, use your readings to look up the relative humidity. The total amount of moisture in the air is called its "absolute" humidity. But the warmer air is, the more water vapor it can hold—so warm air may hold a lot of water, but still seem dry. Relative humidity is the amount of moisture in the air relative to the total amount it could hold.

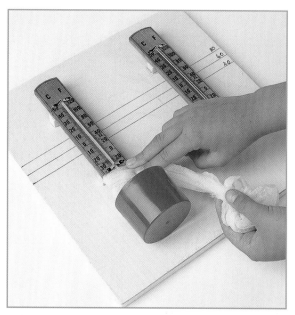

3 Stick the thermometers and the lid to the board so one of the bulbs is in the lid. Wind damp cloth around the bulb.

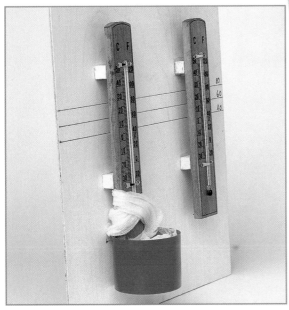

What is happening?

The bulb at the base of one thermometer is in the damp cloth. As the water evaporates from the cloth, it cools the bulb down, so it always gives a slightly lower temperature reading than the other thermometer. In humid weather there will be less evaporation than in dry weather.

2 Mark the scale right across the board. Glue a strip of balsa wood to the back edge of the board to make a stand. Glue blocks to the back of the thermometers.

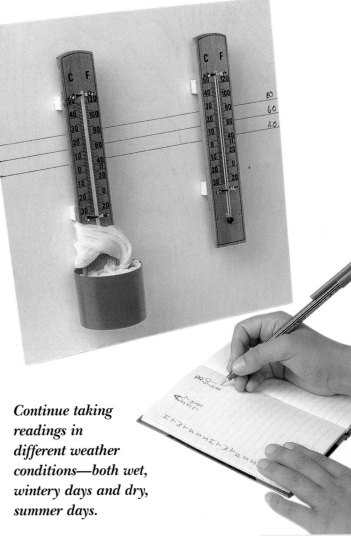

4 Take readings from both thermometers once a day at the same time, and draw a chart to compare the readings.

Continue taking readings in different weather conditions—both wet, wintery days and dry, summer days.

RAIN AND STORMS

Rain is drops of water falling from clouds. But clouds do not always make rain, even though they are full of tiny water droplets and ice crystals.

Most of the droplets in clouds are so tiny and light that they float on air. It only rains when these droplets grow at least a hundred times bigger than normal and get so heavy the air can no longer hold them up.

Cloud drops grow big enough to fall as rain when air is forced to rise suddenly and cools so much that lots of water condenses. Air is forced to rise enough to make rain in three

Lightning occurs when electrical charges build up in clouds and then discharge, like a static shock from metal furniture on a giant scale.

Did you know?

The wettest places in the world are Tutunendo in Colombia and Mount Waialeale, Hawaii, where they get, on average, 460 in (1,170 cm) of rain a year. This would be enough to flood the region deeper than a two-storey house if the water collected!

main ways: on rising currents of warm air; by being forced up over wedges of warm air at a "front"; and when it runs up against hills and mountains.

The faster that air is driven upward, the heavier the rain will be. The heaviest rain comes from giant cumulonimbus clouds created by strong upward currents of warm air, as seen on hot summer afternoons, especially in the tropics. The layered nimbostratus clouds found along "warm" fronts, on the other hand, tend to give long showers of steady rain.

Even when forced up sharply, the water drops do not fall as rain straight away. First they have to grow even bigger. In warm tropical clouds, they grow by colliding with each other. In cooler clouds, they may start as ice crystals that attract water to them to form snow flakes. The flakes fall into warmer air and melt, then fall as rain.

In focus

MAKING RAINDROPS

Cloud droplets only fall as rain when they become big enough to overcome air resistance. You can see how this happens very simply by spraying water on a window pane or mirror. The droplets will cling on to the glass and not run down until they are large enough. Here the obstacle is surface tension. In a cloud it is air resistance.

Use a liquid spray to mist water evenly over a window pane or mirror. At first the drops are small and create a mist.

As you continue to spray, you will see the water start to form rivers as the drops join together and run down the glass.

HOW TO MEASURE RAINFALL

You will need

- ✔ A 2-pint (1-liter) plastic soft drink bottle with straight sides
- ✔ Small plastic bottle, such as a shampoo bottle
- ✔ Marker pen and ruler
- ✔ Measuring cup
- ✔ Scissors
- ✔ Stones

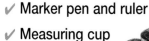

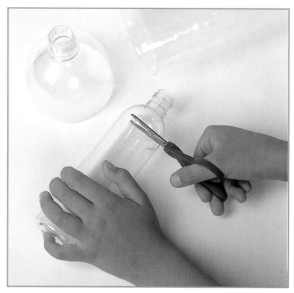

1 Cut the top off the soft drink bottle in a straight line with the scissors: cut around the bottle below the point where it starts to taper. Cut the top off the shampoo bottle.

3 Fill the bottle to the second mark and measure the amount. The difference between these two amounts is the equivalent of ½ in (1 cm) of rain.

4 Pour the measured ½ in (1 cm) into the shampoo bottle and mark the level. Add the same amount of water and make another mark. Repeat up the bottle.

2 Mark a line on the shampoo bottle above the base. Make another mark ½ in (1 cm) higher up. Fill the bottle to the lower mark. Measure the amount of water.

What is happening?

The lid of the bottle acts as a funnel and prevents the rainwater from evaporating before you have taken a reading. Compare your readings with the figures given by the professionals for your region. If your figures are different, see if you can find out why.

5 Place a layer of stones in the large bottle. Stand the small bottle upright in the stones. Turn the top of the large bottle upside down to make a funnel.

6 Stand the rain gauge outdoors, 1 ft (30 cm) above the ground. Check the level of water in the small bottle daily, then empty it. Record the daily rainfall.

HOW TO CREATE LIGHTNING

You will need

✔ A non-conducting board or work surface

✔ Two tin lids or metal plates

✔ Thick polyethylene sheet

✔ Re-usable poster putty

✔ Adhesive tape

1 Use the masking tape to fix each corner of the polyethylene sheet to a surface so that it is stretched out flat.

What is happening?

By rubbing a metal lid on polyethylene you create a static electric charge between the two, just like the electric charge that builds up in cloud particles. When you hold another metal object close to the first, a spark is created that is like a tiny bolt of lightning.

2 Stick a lump of re-usable poster putty centrally inside one lid or dish. This acts as an insulated handle.

THUNDER AND LIGHTNING

Huge thunderclouds are formed by strong updrafts on a hot day or along a cold front. Eddies in the cloud hurl water droplets and ice crystals together, which makes the particles become charged with static electricity. Some particles have positive charges, and others have negative charges. The positive particles gather high in the cloud and negative particles lower down.

After a while, the difference between the positive charge at the top of the cloud and the negative charge at the bottom of the cloud builds up so much that a bolt of electricity—that is, lightning—leaps from positive to negative.

Sometimes this happens within the cloud, giving sheet lightning. Sometimes, though, the lightning leaps from the cloud to the ground, which is also slightly positively charged. This gives forked lightning, which can heat up the air so much that it expands explosively, with a clap of thunder.

3 Touching only the poster putty, rub the lid vigorously over the polyethylene sheet, pressing firmly down.

4 Bring the second lid or dish to within about ¼ in (6 mm) of the first lid. There will be a tiny spark of electricity.

Experiments in Science

Science is about knowledge: it is concerned with knowing and trying to understand the world around us. The word comes from the Latin word, *scire*, to know.

In the early 17th century, the great English thinker Francis Bacon (1521–1626) suggested that the best way to learn about the world was not simply to think about it, but to go out and look for yourself—to make observations and try things out. Ever since then, scientists have tried to approach their work with both observation and experiment. Scientists insist that an idea or theory must be thoroughly tested before it is widely accepted.

All the experiments in this book have been tried before, and the theories behind them are widely accepted. But that is no reason why you should accept them. Once you have done all the experiments in this book, you will know the ideas are true not because we have told you so, but because you have seen for yourself.

All too often in science there is an external factor interfering with the result which the scientist just has not thought of. Sometimes this can make the experiment seem to work when it has not, as well as making it fail. One scientist conducted lots of demonstrations to show that a clever horse called Hans could count things and tap out the answer with his hoof. The horse was indeed clever, but later it was found that rather than counting, he was getting clues from tiny unconscious movements of the scientist's eyebrows.

This is why it is very important when conducting experiments to be as rigorous as you possibly can. The more casual you are, the more "eyebrow factors" you will let in. There will always be some things that you cannot control. But the more precise you are, the less these are likely to affect the outcome.

What went wrong?

However careful you are, your experiments may not work. If so, you should try to find out where you went wrong. Then repeat the experiment until you are absolutely sure you are doing everything right. Scientists learn as much, if not more, from experiments that go wrong as those that succeed. In 1929, Alexander Fleming (1881–1955) discovered the first antibiotic drug, penicillin, when he noticed that a bacteria culture he was growing for an experiment had gone moldy—and that the mold seemed to kill the bacteria. A poor scientist would probably have thrown the moldy culture away. A good scientist is one who looks for alternative explanations for unexpected results.

Glossary

Absorption: The opposite of radiation—the soaking up of light, heat, sound, and other forms of energy. Whenever light strikes a surface, the surface absorbs some of the light and reflects the rest.

Anemometer: Instrument for measuring the wind speed.

Atmosphere: Layer of gases that surrounds Earth.

Barometer: Instrument for measuring the atmospheric pressure.

Beaufort scale: Used to measure wind speed. It ranges from 0 (calm) to 12 (hurricane force).

Equator: Imaginary line around the center of the Earth midway between the North and South Poles.

Evaporation: When a liquid turns into a vapor.

Front: Dividing line between two different air masses.

Humidity: Amount of moisture in the air.

Hurricane: Severe tropical storm that forms over warm oceans with winds of up to 75 mph (120 km/h) around a still center.

Hygrometer: Instrument for measuring humidity.

Infrared: Light waves just too long for our eyes to see. This is the energy given off by hot objects.

Lightning: Discharge of electricity within a cloud, between clouds, or from a cloud to the ground. Often accompanied by thunder.

Pressure: Atmospheric pressure is the force exerted by the atmosphere per unit of area; measured in newtons per m^2 or inches (mm) of mercury.

Radiation: The movement of photons and other subatomic particles (particles within an atom).

Season: Period of the year. The seasons have different kinds of weather based on the amount of sunlight that reaches Earth.

Solar constant: Amount of heat energy that reaches Earth from the Sun.

Thermal: Column of warm, rising air.

Thermometer: Instrument for measuring temperature.

Tornado: Column of air that twists in the vortex around a very low pressure center. Also called a twister or dust devil. Tornadoes are the fastest winds on Earth.

Trade winds: Dry winds that blow in the tropics from the southeast and the northeast toward the equator.

Typhoon: Tropical storm in the western Pacific Ocean.

Index